1/on Scholastic 19⁰⁰

My Birthday Cake

Written by Olivia George

Illustrated by Martha Avilés

children's press®

A Division of Scholastic Inc.
New York Toronto London Auckland Sydney
Mexico City New Delhi Hong Kong
Danbury, Connecticut

Library of Congress Cataloging-in-Publication Data

George, Olivia.
  My birthday cake / written by Olivia George ; illustrated by Martha Avilés.
      p. cm. — (My first reader)
  Summary: A little girl designs herself a birthday cake that has all her favorite ingredients, including jelly beans, cookies, muffins, lollipops, and more.
  ISBN 0-516-25178-3 (lib. bdg.)   0-516-25276-3 (pbk.)
  [1. Cake—Fiction. 2. Birthdays—Fiction. 3. Stories in rhyme. 4. Humorous stories.] I. Avilés Junco, Martha, ill. II. Title. III. Series.
  PZ8.3. G2945My 2005
  [E]—dc22

                                                                    2004010112

Text © 2005 Nancy Hall, Inc.
Illustrations © 2005 Martha Avilés
All rights reserved.
Published in 2005 by Children's Press, an imprint of Scholastic Library Publishing.
Published simultaneously in Canada.
Printed in the United States of America.

1 2 3 4 5 6 7 8 9 10 R 14 13 12 11 10 09 08 07 06 05

Note to Parents and Teachers

Once a reader can recognize and identify the 50 words used to tell this story, he or she will be able to successfully read the entire book. These 50 words are repeated throughout the story, so that young readers will be able to recognize the words easily and understand their meaning.

The 50 words used in this book are:

a	cake	jelly	sweet
about	cherries	know	the
all	chocolate	learned	things
always	cookies	like	to
and	day	lollipops	today
baking	doughnuts	made	too
be	eat	make	want
beans	favorite	Mother's	way
berries	have	my	what
big	hooray	neat	will
birthday	I	new	yummy
blue	is	not	
brownies	it	something	

Today is my birthday.

Hooray! Hooray!

My birthday is
always my favorite day.

I want something yummy.

I know what to make!

I want to make
a big birthday cake!

My cake will be yummy.

My cake will be sweet.

My cake will have
all the things I like to eat!

My cake will have cookies and
chocolate and berries.

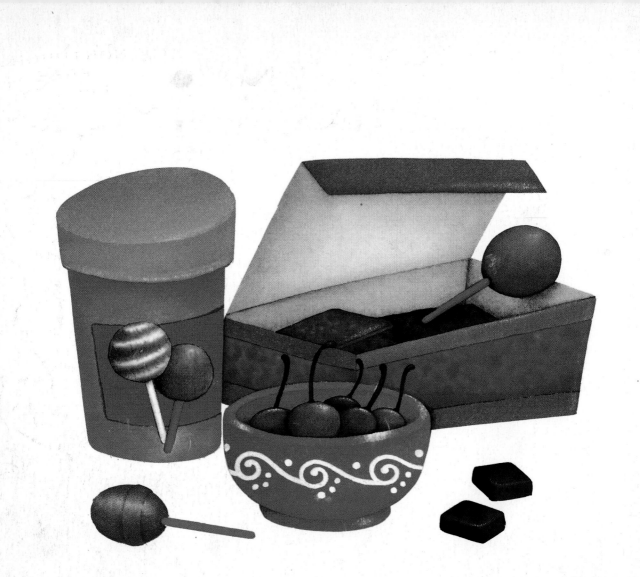

My cake will have lollipops,
brownies, and cherries.

My cake will have doughnuts
and jelly beans, too.

My cake will be yummy.

My cake will be blue!

My cake is too blue!

My cake is not neat!

My cake is too big.

It is too sweet to eat!

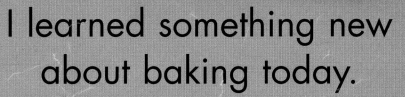

I learned something new
about baking today.

THE
CALIFORNIA
MISSIONS

THE
CALIFORNIA
MISSIONS

—▸✦◂—

**ELIZABETH
VAN STEENWYK**

A First Book
Franklin Watts
New York/Chicago/London/Toronto/Sydney

Cover photograph copyright ©: Ben Klaffke
Photographs copyright ©: Ben Klaffke: pp. 2, 18, 28, 35, 38, 41, 45, 49, 53; North
Wind Picture Archives: pp. 8, 10, 11, 32, 47; The Bettmann Archive: pp. 13, 44;
University of Southern California Library: p. 14; Archive Photos: pp. 16 (American
Stock), 21; Hubert A. Lowman: pp. 24, 27; Mission San Luis Rey Museum: p. 30;
San Diego Historical Society, Photograph Collection: p. 39.

Library of Congress Cataloging-in-Publication Data

Van Steenwyk, Elizabeth.
The California missions / Elizabeth Van Steenwyk.
p.   cm. — (A First book)
Includes bibliographical references and index.
ISBN 0-531-20187-2 (lib. bdg.)
1. Indians of North America—Missions—California—Juvenile literature.
2. Missions—California—History—Juvenile literature.   3. Church architecture—
California—Juvenile literature.   4. Spain—Colonies—America—Administration—
Juvenile literature.   [1. Indians of North America—Missions—California.
2. Missions—California—History.] I. Title. II. Series.
E78.C15V14 1995
979.4'02—dc20   95–3847 CIP AC

CONTENTS

Introduction
A SACRED EXPEDITION
7

The Founding of the Missions

Chapter One
THE MISSIONS BEGIN
12

Chapter Two
THE WORK CONTINUES
23

Chapter Three
THE MISSIONS MARCH ON
31

Mission Life

Chapter One
HOMEMADE MISSIONS
36

Chapter Two
LIFE INSIDE THE MISSIONS
43

Chapter Three
SECULARIZATION AND RESTORATION
51

A MISSION TIMELINE
55

A GLOSSARY OF SPANISH TERMS
57

FOR FURTHER INFORMATION
59

FOR FURTHER READING
61

INDEX
62

A SACRED
EXPEDITION

In 1493, shortly after Christopher Columbus returned to Spain from his first voyage of discovery, the leader of the Roman Catholic Church, Pope Alexander VI, divided the Americas into two spheres of exploration. He assigned all the land west of the dividing line, including the newly discovered "Indies," to Spain and all the land east to Portugal. Then he said that all further explorations be led by "worthy, God-fearing, learned, skilled

7

Christopher Columbus meets with his patrons, King Ferdinand and Queen Isabella. His first voyage of discovery was the beginning of Spanish colonization in America.

and experienced men in order to instruct the inhabitants in the Catholic faith."

During the sixteenth century, Spanish colonizing in the Americas was rapid and successful. It was accomplished with military might and religious zeal in present-day Mexico, Central America, the Caribbean, and part of South America.

The area that was then called California was another matter. Spain laid claim to it when navigator Juan Cabrillo discovered San Diego Bay in 1542. Without established land routes or nearby supply bases, California remained undisturbed for some years. But when Russia and England began to show interest in claiming the land for their own, Spain was moved to action.

In an effort to reestablish claim on Upper or Alta California, the king of Spain, Charles III, ordered the military to secure it for the Crown. In addition, a leader from the Franciscan order of the Catholic Church, Father Junípero Serra, was asked to create a chain of missions to help convert the local Indian peoples to Christianity.

Ultimately, Spain's efforts to colonize and spread Christianity resulted in the building of twenty-one missions along the coastal area of what is now the state of California. All of those missions, in some form of restoration, stand today.

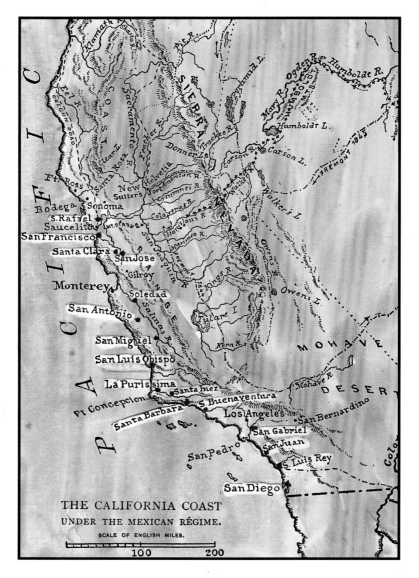

THE CALIFORNIA COAST
UNDER THE MEXICAN RÉGIME.

SCALE OF ENGLISH MILES.

100   200

This early map of the California coast shows only
some of the missions that make up the chain from
San Francisco to San Diego.

The Founding
of the Missions

Chapter

One

THE MISSIONS BEGIN

One day in late June 1769, a dusty mule train from Mexico, or New Spain as it was then called, led by Father Junípero Serra and Gaspar de Portolá, governor of California, neared San Diego Bay. The fifty-five-year-old *padre* was looking forward to reuniting the exploration parties that had left Mexico months before. When everyone gathered, he found that of the 219 original members in the party, only about half were left.

Father Junípero Serra

One ship was lost, many men had deserted or died, and the survivors were ill with scurvy from a lack of fresh fruit and vegetables.

Despite the bleak situation, Father Serra proceeded with plans to build a chain of missions. The *padre*, weak and suffering from an infected leg, roused the remaining men to work. Together, they built an *enramada*, or crude shelter, of brushwood. Then, gray-robed Father

Serra raised the cross within the simple shelter, celebrated Mass, and dedicated *Mission San Diego de Alcala*.

The American Indians who watched from a distance were suspicious of these strangers who arrived in "floating houses" and rode on the backs of unfamiliar animals. The Indians accepted gifts of beads and clothing, but refused offers of food. Before long, they became bold, tried to steal supplies, and even attacked the sick men. A protective stockade was quickly constructed around the crude mission and the Indians were driven away.

After planting the Spanish flag beside the *enramada*, Portolá headed north. He wanted to find Monterey Bay and secure that land for the Crown as well. When he returned to San Diego months later, Portolá was

Gaspar de Portolá, the governor of both Alta (or Upper) and Baja (or Lower) California, led expeditions that paved the way for the establishment of Franciscan missions.

convinced he had failed, but everyone was too weak and hungry to care. Finally, a ship bearing food arrived from Mexico. Within weeks, Father Serra left on the same ship to find the bay Portolá thought he had missed.

Portolá, his men, and another Franciscan friar, Juan Crespí, traveled overland and met the ship bearing Father Serra near where Portolá had placed a cross on his earlier journey. Certain that he had indeed found Monterey Bay, Portolá claimed the land for Spain, and in 1770 the second mission was founded. After bells were hung on some tree branches and an altar erected under a giant oak, uniformed troops and sailors gathered to listen to the *padre* bless the new Spanish mission.

The group soon completed a *presidio*, or fort, and a rustic mission. After turning over military authority to Lieutenant Pedro Fages, Portolá returned to New Spain. Before long, Fages began to interfere with the mission leadership and within months Father Serra had him removed by the viceroy of New Spain, the king's representative there. Fages did return to California later as a governor of the province, but tense relations between the mission's *padres* and military protectors continued.

Within a year, without enough land or water for irrigation, Father Serra moved the Monterey Bay mission to beautiful Carmel Valley, "two gunshots" or 2,400 to 2,800 feet (730 to 850 m) from the sea. It

Also known as the Carmel mission, Mission San Carlos Borromeo has two unusual architectural features for a mission: a domed bell tower (left side) and an arched, instead of flat, church ceiling.

became *Mission San Carlos Borromeo del Rio Carmelo* and headquarters for Father Serra. To protect the first two missions better, the Spaniards began colonizing the land between them.

With builders busy at work on a mission in Carmel, Father Serra set out to find a spot in the Santa Lucia Mountains that Portolá had seen months earlier. After a strenuous hike of 25 Spanish leagues or approximately 75 miles (120 km), Serra and his party stopped in a wooded area near a river, which he named Rio de San Antonio. On a summer day in 1771, Father Serra dedicated *Mission San Antonio de Pádua.* That day many Indians, friendly and eager to help, approached the rustic hut with acorns, pine nuts, and seeds.

Two weeks later, Father Serra returned to Carmel, leaving two other friars in charge of the newest mission. One of them, Father Buenaventura Sitjar, remained for thirty-seven years, during which time he directed the building of an aqueduct to tranport water from a river some miles away, a water-powered mill, and even a fountain. He also wrote a four-hundred-page vocabulary manual of the Mitsun language, spoken by the local Indian population.

Although Father Serra chose the site of the next mission, *Mission San Gabriel Arcángel,* two other *padres* actually dedicated it. During their trip from San Diego, the *padres* and their men met angry Indians. Hoping to prevent an attack, one of the holy men displayed a ban-

This ornate statue of the Virgin Mary from an altar in Mission San Gabriel Arcángel was brought from Spain in 1791.

ner of the Virgin Mary. The Indians dropped their weapons and placed bead necklaces before it. Greatly relieved, the founding party quickly moved on, built a shelter near a stream, and founded a mission in September 1771.

When spring floods ruined crops four years later, Father Fermín Francisco de Lasuén moved the mission to its present site. The mission was soon producing

profitable crops of grain and grapes and serving as a stopping-off place for the frequent visitors who traveled the nearby trails. It became known as the "The Queen of the Missions."

It was Portolá's group who unknowingly led Father Serra to the site of the fifth mission. During their search for Monterey Bay in 1769, they came upon a grassy valley and hordes of grizzly bears looking for food. After feasting on some of the bears, the men named the area La Cañada de los Osos (Valley of the Bears). Soon, a hunting party from the missions came to the valley to scout for food. The hunters later sent back several tons of bear meat to the needy missions. Passing through on his way to San Diego, Father Serra chose for a mission site the valley where food was so plentiful and the Indians friendly. He dedicated *Mission San Luis Obispo de Tolosa* near two streams.

While looking for Monterey Bay in 1769, Portolá stumbled onto San Francisco Bay. After recognizing the importance of the discovery, the viceroy of New Spain resolved to build a *presidio* and send families to settle it for Spain. Lieutenant Colonel Juan Bautista de Anza, who had traveled the deserts and mountains of Upper or Alta California, led an overland party with Father Francisco Palou as its religious leader. On the return trip, De Anza brought four new passengers. The San Diego and San Gabriel missions, overrun with mice, had requested two cats each.

On June 29, 1776, five days before the Declaration of Independence was adopted, Father Palou offered the first Mass at *Mission San Francisco de Asis*. De Anza discovered a nearby stream and named it Arroyo de los Dolores and soon the mission became known as Mission Dolores.

The blustery and chilly climate of the location was not ideal for people or farming. In 1782, Father Palou moved the mission and the city of San Francisco grew up around it. When the earthquake of 1906 hit, the mission remained standing while larger and stronger buildings tumbled to the ground.

Mission San Juan Capistrano was founded twice. The first effort was abandoned because of conflicts with Indians at the San Diego mission. Father Serra headed the second founding party, erected a small chapel, and dedicated it on an autumn day in 1776.

The small house of worship was soon outgrown and an extension was completed in 1806. Only six years later, an earthquake reduced the huge building to rubble in minutes. The tired missionaries and their followers returned to the original chapel and left the great pile of ruin as a testimony to nature's power. The Serra Chapel is thought to be the only surviving structure in California where Father Serra led services.

The viceroy of New Spain ordered the missionaries to build a second San Francisco Bay mission to ward off attacks. *Mission Santa Clara de Asis* was the first named

This corridor of ancient arches and weathered tiles is located alongside the Serra Chapel at Mission San Juan Capistrano.

after a woman, St. Clare of Assissi, the founder of an order of nuns who took vows of absolute poverty. When the settlers found a rapidly flowing creek near the Guadalupe River, about 40 miles (64 km) southeast of Mission Dolores, they built an *enramada* and dedicated the eighth mission in January 1777.

Father Serra had long been eager to establish a third mission between San Diego and Carmel near the Santa Barbara Channel, but he had to wait more than

twelve years. The reason for the delay reached all the way back to Spain, which was involved in costly European wars at the time. The king lacked the funds to support the *padres* and their missions and concluded that white settlers could colonize as easily and more cheaply. After several talks in Mexico City, Father Serra finally convinced Governor Felipe de Neve to approve two more missions and one *presidio*.

The first agreed-upon mission was dedicated on Easter Sunday morning in 1782, with Mass sung by the frail, elderly Father Serra. *Mission San Buenaventura* was successful from the beginning and had crops so abundant that whaling ships stopped regularly to take on cargoes of fruits and vegetables.

Although the *presidio* at Santa Barbara was built without delay, construction of the second mission was more complicated. Governor de Neve felt that the system gave too much power to the *padres* and blocked economic support for another mission. Father Serra waited anxiously for work to begin, but nothing happened. Sadly, he returned to Carmel. Finally, the viceroy reversed the governor's decision and approved funding for *Mission Santa Bárbara*. On August 28, 1784, a month after hearing that the tenth mission would be built after all, Father Serra died.

Chapter

Two

THE WORK CONTINUES

Father Lasuén became the next president of the missions and vowed to finish the work Father Serra had begun. His first project, the mission at Santa Bárbara, was dedicated on December 4, 1786. The mission attracted so many Indian settlers that extra buildings were built and it was soon a small village, with the most complete water system of all the missions. In fact, the city of Santa Barbara still uses the reservoir and dam today.

This statue from Mission San Gabriel Arcángel illustrates the relationship between the padres and their Indian followers. This relationship could be interpreted as caring and paternal or harsh and oppressive.

Father Lasuén dedicated the eleventh mission, *Mission La Purísima Concepción* in December 1787, less than three months after the signing of the U.S. Constitution. The mission thrived in the fertile valley until a tremendous earthquake in 1812 completely shattered the church and nearby buildings. The *padres* quickly built a finer mission some miles away from the old site. Drought, fire, and revolt by some Indians contributed to the mission's decline. Soon, only a few fragments of wall remained to remind anyone a mission once stood there.

The next mission, *Mission Santa Cruz*, was dedicated in 1791. With a favorable location, rich soil, and a warm climate, it seemed set to succeed, but for many reasons, never did.

Although Spanish law forbade *pueblos* to be within one league or roughly 3 miles (5 km) of a mission, Branciforte, named after the viceroy, was settled across the river from the mission. More troubling, the *pueblo* was home to dishonest settlers who stole freely from the missions. One day, the ship of a notorious pirate, Hyppolyte de Bouchard, who had attacked settlements as near as Monterey, was sighted offshore. The *padres* rushed to pack the mission's valuables and store them inland. The citizens of Branciforte, instead of helping, looted the mission. After the pirate ship had passed and the *padres* returned, they found little left for their community. Its converts and religious leaders disheartened, the mission faded away.

During Portolá's search for Monterey Bay in 1769, he came across yet another site for a mission. He and his weary men camped in a dry, desolate spot near the Salinas River and soon learned why the area was so uninhabited. In fact, when an Indian was asked his name, his answer sounded like *soledad*, the Spanish word for "loneliness." It fit the locale and when Father Lasuén dedicated the mission in 1791, he named it *Mission Nuestra Señora de la Soledad*, or Our Lady of Solitude.

Mission life at Our Lady of Solitude proceeded at a leisurely pace. It took six years to build a permanent church and with so few Indians in the area, the population grew slowly. After the *padres* learned how to use the Salinas River for irrigating crops and feeding the animals, life improved. Then a widespread epidemic, floods, and bad weather brought despair to the mission community and many left altogether. The mission roofs were sold to pay a debt to the Mexican government. Soon, only crumbling remnants of the mission remained.

Finally, Father Lasuén appealed to the viceroy of New Spain to fund the missions. He argued that it was less expensive to support missions than military escorts for supply caravans to and from California. The government agreed and authorized money to build five new missions.

The first one, *Mission San José de Guadalupe*, was dedicated on a site east of the southern tip of San Francisco Bay in 1797. Soon cattle and sheep arrived

These are the remains of the massive stone walls that were once part of the original Mission Nuestra Señora de la Soledad.

from the Santa Clara Mission and the small group held a fiesta and a barbecue to celebrate.

Only thirteen days after dedicating the San José mission, Father Lasuén founded the *Mission San Juan Bautista*. Unfortunately, the mission sat on a major fracture of the San Andreas fault. When an earthquake leveled the church, it had to be rebuilt. Almost immediately, plans were made to replace it with a larger church.

Tireless Father Lasuén founded a third mission in the summer of 1797. Attendance was high and fifteen Indian children were baptized at the dedication of

Fresco painting is an art form in which artists apply paint directly to fresh plaster. This fresco at Mission San Miguel Arcángel is seen as it was originally painted; it has never been restored.

Mission San Miguel Arcángel, which immediately prospered. One *padre*, Father Juan Martin, taught the local artisans to make bricks for the new church. When it was finished, a Spanish artist, Esteban Munras, designed and painted the interior including the *reredos*, or wall behind the altar. The San Miguel Church is considered to be the only mission containing its original artwork.

At sixty-one years old, Father Lasuén set to work on building his fourth mission in a four-month period

in 1797. The new mission was located in a valley called Encino, near the growing *pueblo* of Los Angeles. It closed the gap between the San Gabriel and San Buenaventura missions along *El Camino Reál*, which is Spanish for "The Royal Road." *Mission San Fernando Rey de España* flourished after its founding in September.

Later, after gold was discovered on the property, settlers searched for the "dead monks'" treasure in their spare time. When gold was discovered in 1848 at Sutter's Mill in central California, prospectors rushed north and the hunt for gold in the San Fernando mission district was abandoned. The city of Los Angeles, however, expanded and attracted visitors. The mission was soon popular as a convenient overnight stop and rooms were added to accommodate travelers who brought tales of adventure and excitement to the isolated mission.

The ninth and final mission that Father Lasuén founded, *Mission San Luis Rey de Francia*, in 1798, closed the gap between San Diego and San Juan Capistrano. At over 6 acres (2 ha), it occupied the most area, and served the largest population of all the missions. The mission's growth was credited to Father Antonio Peyri, who was present at the founding ceremony and stayed for thirty-four years.

Energetic and organized, Father Peyri was able to bring projects to completion swiftly. A unique water system supported a bathing pond and *lavandería*, or

This photograph of Mission San Luis Rey was taken in 1892. The foundations of Father Peyri's water system and lavandería are in the foreground.

laundry, built below the mission and from which water flowed to irrigate the fields. Father Peyri also directed the planting of fruit trees, vegetable gardens, and vineyards, and the building of a winery.

When Father Peyri left the mission, tradition has it that five hundred mission Indians followed him to San Diego to beg him to come back. They arrived as he was sailing out of the harbor, but he blessed them from his ship. He returned to Spain, knowing that mission life in California as he knew it would soon end.

THE MISSIONS
MARCH ON

The year after Father Lasuén's death in 1803, his successor, Father Estévan Tápis, founded *Mission Santa Inés*, the third dedicated to a woman. Built in a beautiful valley 45 miles (72 km) northwest of the Santa Barbara mission, it was called the "hidden gem of the missions" because visitors had to climb rocky, dusty hills to reach it. The original church, completed in

The missions, usually no more than a comfortable day's horseback ride apart, were convenient gathering places for those traveling up or down the California coast.